To Janice,

I hope you enjoy the story of this special neighborhood that is a warmly remembered part

D1441659

Best Wishes,

Fred Tenley

This Camp Anza matchbook cover was found and purchased on the Internet by the author. It became the inspiration to investigate more about this artifact and the World War II U.S. Army camp from which it came. The result is this book. (Courtesy Frank Teurlay.)

ON THE COVER: The Camp Anza band is shown in formation in front of the camp headquarters building. This building still stands today on Philbin Avenue between Rutland Avenue and Challen Street. (Courtesy Frank Teurlay.)

IMAGES
of America

RIVERSIDE'S CAMP ANZA AND ARLANZA

Frank Teurlay

ARCADIA
PUBLISHING

Published by Arcadia Publishing
Charleston SC, Chicago IL, Portsmouth NH, San Francisco CA

Printed in the United States of America

Library of Congress Catalog Card Number: 2008926300

For all general information contact Arcadia Publishing at:
Telephone 843-853-2070
Fax 843-853-0044
E-mail sales@arcadiapublishing.com
For customer service and orders:
Toll-Free 1-888-313-2665

Visit us on the Internet at www.arcadiapublishing.com

*Dedicated to the residents of Arlanza, past, present, and future,
and the civilian and military personnel who served
at or passed through Camp Anza.*

CONTENTS

ACKNOWLEDGMENTS

Any endeavor, such as this attempt at authoring a book, is really the result of a collaboration of many people whose time, talents, and input are invaluable to the author. There are many who deserve my thanks for contributing various elements ranging from family heirlooms to a simple, kind, listening ear. While there are far too many to list here, the following people have been especially helpful to me: Fred and Louise Woodard; Clara Teurlay; Paul Wormser, director of the National Archives and Records Administration, Laguna Nigel, and his staff; William Swafford and Dominique McCafferty, local history librarians, and the helpful staff of the Riverside Public Library; James K. Herbert; Mary Frances Herbert; Pam Skumawitz; Al Hawkins; Lina Martinez; Phyllis Santomatos; Elaine Ferrari-Santhon; Theresa and Will Breezmeister; Erin Gettis; Steve Lech; Ruby Gwin; Lorene Sisquoc; Randy Stambook; Donna Golden; Joe St. George; Mars Macias; Frank "Bud" Holznagle; Leo Lueras; Peggy Brunner; Judi Bonnett; Janice, John, Phillip and Jean Schuler; Mark Weekly; Dennis Webber; Ruby Jordan; Dennis Jordan; Carol and Ted Burkhart; Ellen Mooney Cryder; Marilyn and Dick Garton; Mary Whaley; the helpful people at Arcadia Publishing, Debbie Seracini, Devon Weston, and Scott Davis; and the kind people in line and behind the counter at Starbucks and Safeway Encina in Walnut Creek, California. Special kudos to my wife, Valerie, and to my children, Elizabeth and Benjamin, for enduring Daddy's latest "mania." To you all and those not named here, but who were of help to me, please accept my heartfelt thanks. This book would not have been possible without you.

The research on Camp Anza and Arlanza will continue. If you have images or artifacts of Camp Anza or early Arlanza, or if you know a veteran, you can assist the author by sending an email to Camp_Anza@pacbell.net.

The majority of the images used in this book are presented courtesy of the National Archives and Records Administration, Laguna Nigel (NARA). Images from other sources are credited accordingly.

INTRODUCTION

Growing up in the Arlanza District of Riverside, California, in the 1960s was a far different experience than growing up in today's world. I was fortunate to experience a time when people did not lock their doors. A bicycle could be left out in the front yard overnight and still be there in the morning. We had not heard of such a thing as a bike lock. A child might walk out the door in the morning to play with friends and not return until after dark without causing his parents to panic. There were no cell phones in those days to stay in contact. They weren't needed. It was a carefree time.

If we young baby boomers weren't out exploring the undeveloped areas of the neighborhood, we were watching Westerns and World War II movies on television. We reenacted these scenes when playing out at Hidden Lake or during recess at school. There was nothing more fun than being part of a group of boys on a cavalry charge to rescue the wagon train from the "Injuns" or going on a mission to retake a hill from the "Japs," just as we had watched our heroes do on television.

While at play, we would come across old buildings or foundations that, at the time, seemed to have been ancient. I recall coming across what appeared to be a swimming pool behind the Arlanza Elementary School playground. It was overgrown with weeds. I wondered who swam there and how many centuries ago they did so. Whenever I hit a baseball over my backyard fence, I had to walk down to Arlington Avenue, head east, and knock on the door of an imposing, creepy, old wooden building that guarded the entrance of a place called Girl's Town. I would ask permission to go back to the area where ponies were kept at one time to retrieve my ball. With permission granted, I wandered down a path past old buildings and what appeared to be untended vineyards to collect my ball. I often wondered to myself, "if this is Girl's Town, where are the girls? Perhaps they keep them locked up somewhere, perhaps in one of those creepy old buildings?" In all the years of repeating this scenario, I never saw a single girl at Girl's Town. Out near Hidden Lake, we played war games on a vast area under shade trees where large broken chunks of concrete piled high made terrific breastwork fortifications. Little did we know that we were playing out World War II battle scenarios on property that, just 20 years earlier, was used by the U.S. Army to prepare real soldiers to fight real World War II battles in the Pacific.

As the decades passed and youth transformed into adulthood, memories of these precious times faded. As I reached middle age, I grew quite nostalgic for the hometown of my youth. To quell the nostalgic itch, I began collecting vintage Riverside postcards. The images rekindled fond memories of carefree times in Riverside. One day, while searching the Internet for more Riverside postcards, I came upon a matchbook with "Camp Anza" printed on the cover together with the army logo. I thought "if it came up on a search of Riverside, it must have been there at some time." The only military establishment near Riverside I was aware of was March Air Force Base, my birthplace. My mind struggled to make a connection; Camp Anza? Arlanza? Could they somehow be connected? Further research confirmed that there was, in fact, a Camp Anza near Riverside during World War II. Why did I not know that? No one ever talked about an army camp. Was this place lost to history? Was it somehow associated with my neighborhood, Arlanza? I had to know more.

On my next trip to Riverside, I visited the museum and libraries to inquire about books I could read to learn more about this World War II U.S. Army camp. Sadly, there was little available to shed light on Camp Anza. In fact, in the books that do mention the camp at all, the sum total of information amounts to just a few sentences. However, the books did confirm that Camp Anza was located at what later came to be known as Arlanza. Wow! My neighborhood did have roots dating back to World War II. I had to know more. Continued attempts to learn more about Camp Anza indicated that I would have to dig it up myself.

It was a challenge I savored. What fun it would be to learn firsthand what took place in my neighborhood during the pre-Teurlay era. Many hours spent in the library, at the National Archives, and on the Internet paid off. I was able to uncover wonderful stories about the camp, its purpose, and some of the personalities associated with its operation. It was information I wish I had known when growing up there. I would have had a totally different outlook on the neighborhood. I would have understood the context of the old places we came across as children. It soon became one of my goals to share the story of Camp Anza. Pursuit of this goal has been a genuinely rewarding experience. Each week, upon the discovery of a new fact or image, I experienced a joy similar to unwrapping a long-anticipated Christmas gift. I have since opened many such gifts and it is my pleasure to share some of what I have unwrapped in this book.

Research has shown that the old buildings and foundations we found as children were remnants of a World War II U.S. Army camp that existed from 1942 until 1946 in a rural area 6 miles southwest of Riverside known today as the Arlanza District. In 1942, five months after the Japanese surprise attack on Pearl Harbor, 1,200 acres of land used for growing alfalfa were purchased by the government for use as an army staging area. It became known as Camp Anza, named for the Spanish explorer Juan Batista de Anza, whose California expedition passed near the area in 1774. Soon a bustling camp was built that could house up to 20,000 troops at a time.

What I thought was a swimming pool was actually the foundation of the Camp Anza Theater. Bob Hope and Kay Kyser did national radio broadcasts from this location during the war. The creepy buildings that comprised Girl's Town were actually a part of the camp known as the Arlington Reception Center. Desi Arnaz was stationed there for a time. Italian prisoners of war were also housed there. The concrete we used to play war games on was most likely the foundation rubble of demolished Arlington Reception Center buildings. What we called "Hidden Lake" was, in fact, Hole Reservoir, used during World War II to train GIs on the use of lifeboats. The Camp Anza story began to take shape, and I was able to see the adventurous discoveries of my childhood in a totally new light.

Camp Anza was where troops spent their last 10 days on U.S. soil while awaiting deployment overseas to the Pacific theater. Typically the troops would complete basic training at various camps around the United States, then be transported by train to one of several staging areas near a port of embarkation. Camp Anza was the staging area for the Los Angeles Port of Embarkation in Wilmington, California. Upon arrival at Camp Anza, troops would receive immunizations and uniforms appropriate to their assigned destination. They would be given orientation training on the customs, habits, and culture of their destination country, and they would be encouraged and assisted in writing their will before heading out to face the enemy. As time permitted, there was training on the use of gas masks (Camp Anza had the largest gas mask training room in the United States) and lifeboat use, should the abandon-ship order be given while at sea.

To give the departing soldiers a positive environment before leaving the homeland, several recreational opportunities were provided at the camp. Basketball, volleyball, and softball were popular. Hollywood movies were shown nightly, and big-name celebrities often performed at the camp's indoor or outdoor theaters. A few of the notables include, Bob Hope and Desi Arnaz, Harpo and Groucho Marx, Lena Horne, Lucille Ball, Orson Welles, Shirley Temple, the boxer Joe Louis, and athlete Babe Didrikson Zaharias.

Camp Anza had the largest military laundry in the west. It handled all army laundry for a radius of 250 miles. The camp also served as a detention center for German and Italian prisoners of war. The POWs served food in the camp mess halls, and the Italian POWs were allowed to work in the camp laundry. There was a military cooks' and bakers' school at Camp Anza, as well as a butchers' school.

At the end of the war, Camp Anza served as a welcome-home point for troops returning from the Pacific. GIs were only in camp for 24 to 48 hours while their paperwork was put in order and trains were assembled to transport them to their final discharge point. Two illustrious army divisions were welcomed home at Camp Anza. The first was the 38th Infantry Division, known as the "Cyclones." They gained fame as the "Avengers of Bataan." This moniker became an official part of their name after liberating the Bataan peninsula in the Philippines. This was appreciated as revenge by the public in the U.S. after the tragic Bataan Death March in 1942. The second famous division to pass through Camp Anza was the 96th, known as the "Deadeyes." They earned respect for gallant fighting in the last and bloodiest land battle of World War II, Okinawa. Okinawa was the final Pacific island objective for U.S. military forces before an anticipated invasion of the home islands of Japan. The fighting was fierce, as brave Japanese soldiers fought to the death, knowing that they alone stood between Allied forces and their homeland and families.

It was at Camp Anza that war-weary GIs got their first real taste of home. While in camp, soldiers received a steak dinner with all the trimmings, milk shakes, and a phone call home to speak with loved ones for the first time in months or even years. They were issued new Class A uniforms and got to sleep in a bed with sheets and a pillow for the first time in what must have seemed an eternity. These were special treats to GIs who had gone without for so long. A barracks bunk was heaven on earth compared to sleeping in a foxhole while undergoing constant mortar fire.

On March 31, 1946, Camp Anza was officially closed. The War Assets Department placed the former Camp Anza property up for sale. The Anza Realty Company purchased the property and began selling parcels for development. Two of the early buyers were Rohr Corporation, headquartered in Chula Vista, California, and Burpee Seed Company, headquartered in Philadelphia, Pennsylvania. Rohr built a plant on the south side of Arlington Avenue west of Van Buren Boulevard. In 1963, Rohr's new Space Products Division was created at the Riverside plant, where parts for Titan III rockets were assembled. Burpee Seed Company located its western regional headquarters in the former camp laundry building, located at Arlington and Rutland Avenues. Across the street, along the north side of Arlington Avenue, row upon row of beautiful seed flowers were grown for several years for distribution across the United States.

Beginning in 1948, former barracks were sold as housing. The area between Cypress Avenue and Philbin Avenue to the north and south and Montgomery Street and Rutland Avenue on the east and west still shows its military heritage. Many homes in this area still have the basic barracks profile despite modifications to update them. In the early 1950s, newly constructed housing was completed north of Arlington Avenue and south of Philbin Avenue, resulting in the Arlanza neighborhood we know today.

As housing brought families into the area, a sense of community was established by the residents. I am forever grateful for the dads who taught us how to play baseball and the moms in the stands who cheered us on. Much of the sense of community came from the fact that everyone in the neighborhood had a family member who worked at Rohr or knew someone who did. Each year in March, Rohr would reserve Disneyland for an entire evening for the uncrowded enjoyment of its employees and their families. At Christmas, Rohr reserved the Fox Theater for an afternoon of cartoons and stage shows for the enjoyment of the children of employees. This served a dual purpose. The children had a great afternoon of fun, sometimes hosted by Tom Hatton, host of the popular Popeye cartoon show seen every afternoon on KTLA Channel 5. In addition, it occupied the children for a few hours so that parents had some free time to do Christmas shopping.

In recalling these happy memories of simpler times, it dawned on me that we owe a great deal of gratitude to the generation who built Camp Anza and fought in World War II. Their no-nonsense values were forged in the deprivations of the Great Depression. They went on to win a war that destroyed a very real threat to the way of life and freedoms we take for granted today. After the war, this generation built the homes and infrastructure that are the envy of all the world. They made the baby boomer years of 1950s and 1960s the best period in history in which to be a child. I am glad to have been a part of that time.

The Camp Anza matchbook cover inspired me to embark on a wonderful and rewarding journey of discovery. As a result, I came away with a better understanding of the origins of my neighborhood. It left me with a strong appreciation for the men and women who brought the camp and the neighborhood that followed in its place to life. It is my sincere hope that this Images of America book will prove equally rewarding to the reader.

One

IN THE BEGINNING

At the start of World War II, the U.S. Army's major port on the west coast was in San Francisco. It soon became apparent that more port capacity was required to meet the military's anticipated demand for shipping troops and war material to the Pacific. Ports in Seattle and Los Angeles were designated "sub ports" (meaning subordinate to the San Francisco port, not referring to submarines). Col. William A. Aird was designated as commander of the Los Angeles sub port on January 24, 1942. He stated that, when he first reported for duty, he was the only member of the Los Angeles sub port staff, acting as everything from office boy to commanding officer.

A staging area for troops awaiting shipment to the Pacific was required, but land near the port was scarce. On April 15, 1942, Colonel Aird submitted his report recommending the selection of a 1,200-acre lot southwest of Riverside, California, and approximately 48 miles from the Los Angeles Port of Embarkation (LAPE), as it was now called. This lot was favored because it was relatively flat, undeveloped land close to existing rail lines. Other locations that were considered included Wilmington, Mira Loma, and a lot on the northwest corner of Magnolia and La Sierra Avenues.

Maj. Walter A. Johnson was assigned the task of constructing the staging area. It was first known as the Arlington Staging Area, but was quickly renamed Camp Anza in honor of Juan Bautista de Anza, the famous Spanish explorer. Major Johnson set up an office in the Jenkins Building, at the corner of Magnolia and Van Buren Boulevard, and went to work. By early 1943, Camp Anza was a fully functional staging area. In February 1943, Col. Earle R. Sarles was named commanding officer of Camp Anza. In May of the same year, Col. Abbott Boone was named commander of the LAPE, replacing Colonel Aird. In November 1943, Col. James K. Herbert, executive officer for Maj. Gen. C. P. Gross, chief of the Office of Transportation, was named commander of the LAPE for the duration of the war.

The Cahuilla tribe of Native Americans were likely inhabitants of the area that now comprises Arlanza prior to European colonization. This mural, depicting a typical village, is located in the Rubidoux Nature Center. It reflects how early inhabitants of Arlanza may have lived up to the time of Juan Bautista de Anza's exploration of California. It was painted for the center by Kathie Dillon in 2006. (Courtesy Kathie Dillon and University of California Riverside.)

Juan Bautista de Anza crossed the Santa Ana River in 1774 as he explored an inland trail through current-day California. His crossing took place just northeast of present-day Arlanza. De Anza is immortalized with a statue at the intersection of Market and Fourteenth Streets in downtown Riverside. (Courtesy Frank Teurlay.)

Col. William A. Aird was the first commander of the Los Angeles Port of Embarkation. The port needed a large area for the staging of troops prior to boarding a troop ship for the Pacific. Colonel Aird submitted a report recommending the purchase of a 1,200-acre plot of relatively level, undeveloped land that was close to existing rail lines near Riverside, California. (Courtesy Riverside Public Library.)

Below is Exhibit I of Colonel Aird's report. It is a Department of Interior map showing the proposed location relative to the city of Riverside. The proposed land is shown as two 600-acre parcels identified as Tract A to the south and Tract B to the north. The tracts are bisected by Arlington Avenue just west of Van Buren Boulevard. (Courtesy NARA.)

Col. Wm. A. Aird . . . in Command of L. A. Sub Port

We have finally managed to secure sufficient information about Col. William A. Aird to permit us to make him the main topic of our newspaper for this week. As commanding officer of Los Angeles Sub Port, Col. Aird is also in command of Camp Anza since we are part of the port installation.

Col. Aird was born in Australia and after looking at his picture we are sure it is not necessary to tell you that his parents were both Scotch. He came from a long line of military men, was a cadet in the Australian Military Forces, served in the South African Boer War, and is a graduate of our Military School.

Col. Aird has had a wide and varied military career. At the close of the Boer War he came to the United States and enlisted in the United States Cavalry which is, in his opinion, the best branch of the service. Col. Aird has served in the Philippines, fought in the Battle of Bud Dajo, on the Island of Jolo; served as a first sergeant with the United States Cavalry in Mexico during Francisco I. Madero's Revolution, which overthrew Diaz. He was commissioned in 1916, and organized the 348th Machine Gun Battalion, 91st Wild West Division, in the First World War, and participated in the Battles of St. Mehiel, Meuse Argonne, Ypre, Lye, Belgium. Col. Aird was appointed Military Governor in Germany after the Armistice and

was Ass't. Adjutant General 3rd Army, Army of Occupation, Coblenz, Germany, until the return of the Army of Occupation to the

United States. Col. Aird was Commanding Officer of the 381st Infantry for 19 years. He came to the Los Angeles Harbor from Portland, Oregon, on January 24, 1942, and opened and organized the Los Angeles Sub-Port.

Col. Aird has been decorated with the Distinguished Service Cross, Croix De Guerre, King Edwards Medal, Queen Victoria's Medal, three Campaign Medals and the medal for Army of Occupation in Germany.

The members of Camp Anza salute you, Col. Aird, and consider it an honor and a pleasure to serve in your Command.

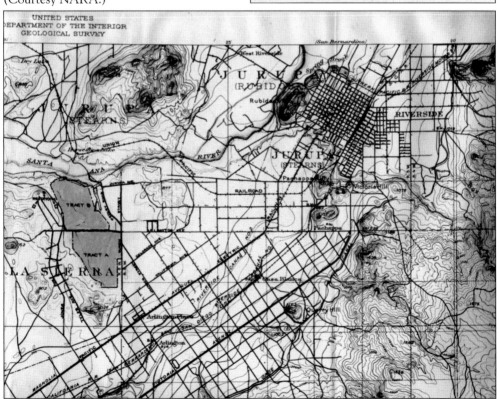

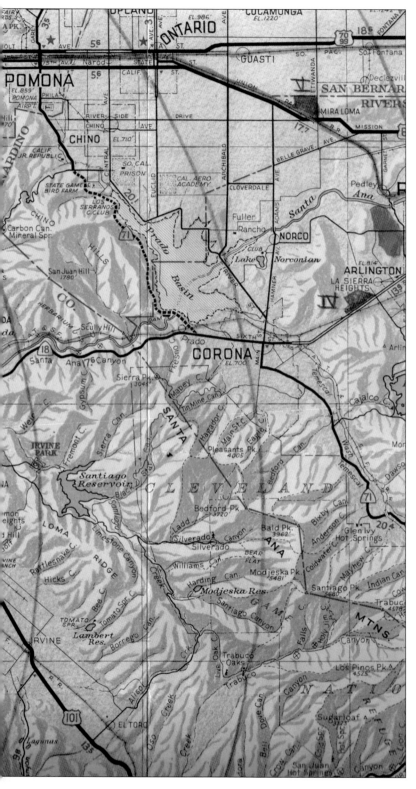

This detail from Exhibit IV of Colonel Aird's April 15, 1942, report shows the LAPE as the epicenter near Wilmington in the lower left of the map. The proposed staging area site appears on the far right, just below the Santa Ana River and above the word "Arlington." The hand-drawn rings represent increments of 10 miles from the LAPE, making the staging area roughly 48 miles from the port. Mira Loma and La Sierra Heights can also be identified as site options. On the original map, rail lines are outlined in colored pencil to show the possible routes from the proposed staging area to the LAPE. (Courtesy NARA.)

The c. 1942 aerial photograph above shows the boundaries of the available land under consideration. The town of Arlington can be seen in the lower center of the image. In the upper right, the Union Pacific Railroad line is shown. The spot where the line crosses the Santa Ana River is where the one-time largest concrete structure in the world, the rail bridge crossing the Santa Ana River, still stands today. A few hundred feet east of this bridge is where Juan Bautista de Anza camped and then crossed the river in 1774. The May 1945 photograph below, facing north, shows Camp Anza late in the war. To the right of the arrow is the station hospital. The arrow points at what today is Rutland Avenue. (Courtesy NARA.)

Maj. Walter A. Johnson (above), who came to be known as the "Father of Camp Anza," was assigned the task of constructing the camp. After beginning without office space, Major Johnson took an office in the Jenkins Building at the corner of Magnolia and Van Buren Boulevard in nearby Arlington. The Jenkins Building appears on the right in the postcard below. When new commanding officer Col. Earle R. Sarles arrived at Camp Anza in early 1943, he paid special tribute to Major Johnson: "[he] truly is the father of our camp. He has built every building . . . established the policy . . . and made Camp Anza . . . a smoothly operating military organization. His sure, quick judgment coupled with an amazing supply of energy is a constant inspiration to every officer and soldier. He did a big job in a big way . . . in a big hurry." (Above, courtesy NARA; below, courtesy Frank Teurlay.)

MAGNOLIA AVE. AND VAN BUREN ST., ARLINGTON, CALIFORNIA

This view shows the camp headquarters in the foreground, flanked by the dentist building on the left and the camp post office on the right. These buildings face Philbin Avenue. Just above the headquarters is the main camp theater, one of four at Camp Anza. To the left of the theater, on what is known today as Challen Street, is the gymnasium. The large building near the right center is the Officer's Club on Picker Street. This building still stands today. Further up, on the extreme far right, is the Service Men's Club. It no longer exists, but stood on Montgomery Street. On the horizon, in the upper center portion of the photograph, is Mt. Rubidoux near downtown Riverside. (Courtesy Riverside Public Library.)

Above, facing northeast, the station hospital appears in the foreground. Just above the hospital complex is Area B showing the mess hall surrounded by barracks. To the right of Area B is Area A, with its own mess hall. The camp headquarters can be seen in the left center of the photograph. Below, looking to the southeast, troops can be seen in line in the left foreground, ready to board a train. The large building in the left center is the Post Exchange (PX) along what is known today as Cypress Avenue. The long narrow building to the left of the PX is the equipment inspection building. Above the inspection building is a medical building. Beyond the PX, Area A is clearly shown. The road beyond Area A is Van Buren Boulevard. In the far upper right is the nearby town of Arlington. (Courtesy Riverside Public Library.)

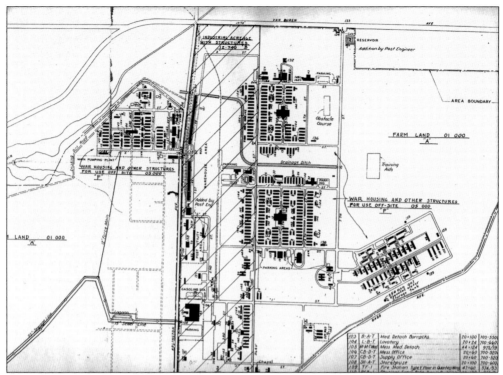

103	B-A-T	Med. Detach Barracks	20x100	700-550
104	L-B-T	Lavatory	20x24	700-660
105	M-M-Tkk	Mess Med. Detach	44x124	975/19
106	CB-D-T	Mess Office	20x60	700-520
107	CB-D-T	Supply Office	20x60	700-520
108	SH-A-T	Storehouse	20x100	700-600
109	YF-1	Fire Station Type Y Flex in Qvarters Wing	47x60	574/33

This map is a detail of the Camp Anza layout. The top faces east toward Van Buren Boulevard. The street bisecting the map is Fourth Street, which is now Cypress Avenue. The major thoroughfare to the left is Arlington Avenue. On the south side of Arlington, two long narrow warehouse buildings can be seen. One still stands as part of the Goodrich Aerostructures property. On the north side of Arlington was the Arlington Reception Center. The large complex of barracks in the center of the map is Area B, with Area A above, nearer to Van Buren. Additional roadways compare to today's Arlanza as follows: present-day Philbin Avenue was Seventh Street; Montgomery Street was B Street; Warren Street was D Street; Picker Street was F Street; Challen Street was H Street; and Rutland Avenue was I Street. (Courtesy NARA.)

Major Snider, camp engineer, is seen pointing to a large map of Camp Anza that was located in the provost office. The area he is pointing is generally the intersection of Cypress Avenue and Picker Street near the main PX. (Courtesy NARA.)

Col. Earle R. Sarles became the commanding officer of Camp Anza on February 9, 1943. A graduate of the University of North Dakota, Colonel Sarles served in World War I. After World War I, Colonel Sarles was a bank president and ran an insurance business. He was described as a genial man by many who met him. (Courtesy NARA.)

On October 29, 1943, Col. James K. Herbert is shown here assuming command of the LAPE, succeeding Col. Abbott Boone. Colonel Herbert attended West Point and served in the Army Corps of Engineers. This photograph was taken in the commanding officer's headquarters office at the LAPE in Wilmington, California. Colonel Herbert was also overall commander of Camp Anza, which was a part of the LAPE. (Courtesy NARA.)

In January 1944, after performing admirably throughout the construction of Camp Anza, Maj. Walter Johnson was promoted to colonel. He is shown in his office in the Camp Anza Headquarters Building. (Courtesy NARA.)

This photograph, taken in the Officer's Club, shows Colonel Sarles and his staff. These officers were responsible for the efficient operation of Camp Anza. From left to right are (first row) Major Speilman, Lieutenant Colonel Johnson, Colonel Sarles, Major Alson, and Major Anderson; (second row) Lieutenant Corn, Captain Wright, Captain Stevens, Captain Slagle, Major Baldridge, Major Cumarelas, and Lieutenant Loughery. (Courtesy the Herbert family.)

Two

CAMP FUNCTIONS
SHIPPING OUT TO WAR

As the staging area for the LAPE, Camp Anza was where soldiers spent their last 10 days on U.S. soil before boarding ship for transport to the Pacific. Basic training for army units passing through Camp Anza was completed elsewhere. Just before shipping out of the LAPE, GIs arrived by train at the staging area. While in camp, troops were encouraged to make out their will and financial arrangements should they die while in service. Assistance in completing the paperwork was provided and was used frequently, given that a significant number of soldiers were uneducated.

Orientation was provided to assist the troops in understanding the war in general and their role in achieving victory. They were given a basic understanding of the customs and culture of the people in the country to which they were being sent. In addition, soldiers were provided uniforms appropriate to the climate of their destination, as well as immunizations specific to the diseases to which they might be exposed.

Final equipment checks were made and some final preparation training was provided at Camp Anza. A soldier could exchange his weapon, no questions asked. The same went for any other piece of equipment right down to minor wear on the heels of his boots. The army wanted every departing GI to feel confident in the equipment he had been issued. While in camp, soldiers learned to climb a rope ladder that might be used in boarding an amphibious landing craft from a ship at sea. Out at Hole Reservoir, on the north boundary of the camp, they were taught how to board and deploy a lifeboat should this task be required at sea. Many GIs did not know how to swim and were given basic swimming lessons at the same location. Camp Anza also boasted the largest gas mask training room in the United States.

When not engaged in these activities, troops were free to utilize the many recreational and entertainment opportunities in camp, but troops awaiting shipment were not allowed to leave the camp.

Cpl. Richard Nickson was the Camp Anza information officer, assigned to the camp's information and education office in the War Information Center. He presented orientation classes for troops bound for foreign destinations and read the latest Associated Press teletype releases over the camp public address system each day at noon. He also contributed to local Riverside radio station KPRO. (Courtesy NARA.)

During an orientation class, Pvt. Vincent Rapp is shown (left) pointing to Japan, the ultimate objective of the Pacific war. The war, its leaders, and current operations were explained to the GIs about to embark to the Pacific to join the fighting. (Courtesy NARA.)

Visual aids made the geography and current issues easier to grasp. Understanding the full context of the war and the GIs' role in winning it was an important part of the full range of training provided to U.S. soldiers during World War II. (Courtesy NARA.)

Here is a view of the Pacific-war orientation display showing the many campaigns and fighting fronts involving U.S. forces. The title of the display is "Here Is Your War." (Courtesy NARA.)

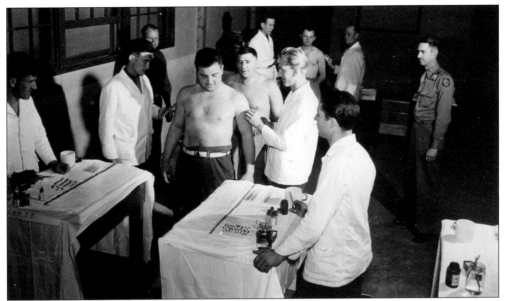

Soldiers shown above are receiving immunizations. Notice that shots are being given in both arms at the same time. When large military units passed through Camp Anza, efficient assembly lines such as this were required to process the volume of troops. At times, doctors from the U.S. Naval Hospital, in nearby Norco, came to Camp Anza to assist in providing inoculations to the GIs. (Courtesy NARA.)

A soldier could turn in his weapon for a new one, no questions asked. A soldier's confidence in his equipment was of utmost importance. As part of orientation, GIs were familiarized with the arms used by the enemy. Shown here is an orientation section showing various Japanese guns, grenades, and clothing. (Courtesy NARA.)

Capt. William O. Strong, from Williamsburg, Virginia, demonstrates the use of a lifeboat at Hole Reservoir at right. The reservoir was built around 1915 by landowner Willits J. Hole to provide irrigation water for his alfalfa and barley fields. During World War II, the reservoir was used by the army to show GIs how to deploy a lifeboat in the event their troop transport ship was torpedoed at sea. The reservoir was also used to provide basic swimming lessons to troops who could not swim. Later GI swim lessons were provided at the nearby Arlington park pool. Below, Sgt James Sullenger readies gas masks for the next training class. Camp Anza had the largest gas mask training building in the United States, capable of handling 250 GIs at one time. (Courtesy NARA.)

Troops march in pairs to the equipment checkroom. The railroad tracks in the foreground are the same ones traveled by the train that brought them into camp. This location is on the western portion of where Goodrich Aerostructures stands today. (Courtesy NARA.)

Here the GIs are shown entering the equipment check building, while a previous unit can be seen exiting the side of the building. This building stood where Rohr Corporation built its "Hall of Giants" in 1963. The current seven-story building that stands on this spot was built to work on space program projects. (Courtesy NARA.)

Once inside the equipment check building, troops were guided through an inspection of all of their issued equipment, including gas masks. This was done so that each soldier would know what has been issued and its proper use. (Courtesy NARA.)

The unit leaves the equipment check building and enters the medical building. The main PX can be seen in the center of the photograph. (Courtesy NARA.)

The debarkation tower was used to train troops to safely climb and descend a rope ladder, as was used by ships at sea in transferring soldiers to amphibious landing craft. There were two such structures at Camp Anza along Philbin Avenue, one near Challen Street and the other near Wohlstetter Street. (Courtesy the Herbert family.)

When the order to ship out was received, army units boarded a train for the LAPE in Wilmington, California. Railroad cars were assigned numbers to assist the GIs in boarding the correct car. Chalk numerals were written on the helmets to facilitate headcounts and space assignments. (Courtesy the Herbert family.)

Troops en route to the port savor their last views of the United States before boarding ship. Many are also seeing the sights of southern California for the first time. (Courtesy the Herbert family.)

While transitioning from the train to their ship, GIs are greeted by Red Cross workers offering coffee and cookies along with a few words of thanks and encouragement for the important task ahead. (Courtesy the Herbert family.)

Before the unit boards ship, final headcounts are made to ensure that no GI is missing and that no unauthorized persons board the troop transport. (Courtesy the Herbert family.)

Once given the go ahead, troops climb the gangplank to enter their floating home for the next few weeks. (Courtesy the Herbert family.)

Once aboard, GIs carry their equipment to their assigned part of the ship. (Courtesy the Herbert family.)

GIs (left) gather around a piano above deck. Singing was one of several activities used to pass the time on the long, tedious journey. The GIs seen here are wearing their "Mae Wests," a nickname for their lifejackets. (Courtesy the Herbert family.)

Quarters were cramped aboard ship, as seen in this view of sleeping quarters. The ship's bunks were stacked four high. GIs often had to share precious space with war cargo, also bound for the Pacific. (Courtesy NARA.)

Space was such a premium that eating areas were designed for meals to be taken standing up. (Courtesy NARA.)

Wounded GIs from the Pacific were cared for at the Camp Anza Station Hospital. While most camp barracks had wooden floors, the hospital wards had nicer flooring and were reported to have been constructed better. After the war, some of these hospital ward buildings were bought by the Riverside School District. They were moved for use as classrooms to various schools around Riverside. (Courtesy NARA.)

This group photograph shows nurses who served at the Camp Anza Station Hospital. (Courtesy NARA.)

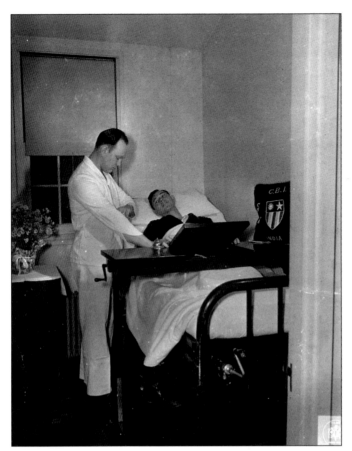

An orderly checks the vital signs of a Camp Anza Station Hospital patient. The "CBI" pillow on the bed may indicate that this GI served in the China Burma India (CBI) theater. (Courtesy NARA.)

The hospital ship *Mercy* was one of three U.S. Navy hospital ships serving in the Pacific and staffed with army nurses. The army nurses assigned to the *Mercy* received training at the Camp Anza Station Hospital before being deployed. (Courtesy the Herbert family.)

Three

LIFE IN CAMP

Camp Anza soon became a small community unto itself. It had all the infrastructure and related maintenance requirements of a small town. Switchboard operators, clerical workers, painters, and carpenters were among the many jobs Camp Anza called on the civilian population to fill. Bond drives were a constant activity to raise the money needed to fund the war effort. Blood drives were also a critical wartime activity to provide for the demands of the station hospital.

The camp had at least four PXs, which had soda fountains and stores to purchase personal items and souvenirs. A large service club provided a place to relax for both military and civilian personnel. During World War II, the military was still segregated, so a separate Colored Service Club, as it was called, was built for African American servicemen. There were weekly dances in the service clubs, to which local young ladies were invited as dance partners for the soldiers. Music was provided by excellent dance bands headed by professional musicians with ties to Hollywood. There was a nicely appointed Officers Club catering to commissioned officers.

Famous entertainers from movies and radio performed for the GIs at both an indoor and an outdoor theater. Entertainment was also provided by amateur talent from the camp or the director of entertainment, Arthur Todd, and his wife, Dotty, who went on to stardom of their own after the war.

Camp Anza provided both intramural and competitive athletic opportunities for the station complement and GIs passing through. The camp's softball team won the army's 9th Service Command championship two years running.

As with any community, there were jobs to be done, love lives to be pursued, and mischief to be made. In every community, babies are conceived (though not always planned), crimes are committed, and sometimes people are murdered. The community of Camp Anza was no different. Working closely together for a period of time often leads to intimate and lifelong relationships. This chapter will cover some of the routines and people at Camp Anza.

Because of the popularity of Mickey Mouse and other Disney characters, the Walt Disney studios were asked to create insignia for several military units during World War II. Here is the design created for the ports of embarkation, which were part of the army's Special Services Division. Happy, from the movie *Snow White and the Seven Dwarfs*, is portrayed as a waiter, ready to serve, as was the Special Services Division. (Courtesy NARA.)

In 1943, the army's Transportation Corps was officially formed, and this shoulder patch was created. It was worn by station complement military personnel at Camp Anza and the LAPE. The colors were cardinal and gold, similar to those of the University of Southern California. (Courtesy NARA.)

Cooks are seen preparing a meal in one of the mess hall kitchens. Area A and Area B each had a large mess hall surrounded by barracks. (Courtesy NARA.)

Here cooks are preparing fried chicken in the kitchen of one of the two main camp mess halls. (Courtesy NARA.)

Seen here is the mess hall serving line. (Courtesy NARA.)

Camp Anza also had a baker and cook school to train personnel to provide meals for thousands of troops at a time. Here bakers are shown using the large ovens in the mess hall kitchen. (Courtesy NARA.)

Pictured here are T4g. Robert Smith and T5g. Reinhold Hoenzch making doughnuts using the camp's doughnut machine. The machine could make 940 doughnuts per hour. As needed, the mess hall could produce 5,000 to 10,000 doughnuts per shift. (Courtesy NARA.)

In the mess hall meat locker, sides of beef are inspected. In addition to the baker and cook school, Camp Anza also had a school for butchers. (Courtesy NARA.)

Pvt. Artie Bourne served as a cook in the Camp Anza mess halls. His niece, Bunny Johnson White, had a pet grooming shop on Cypress after the war. His nephew, Rou Johnson, ran Hogies Pet Shop and Petting Zoo, also on Cypress. (Courtesy Bunny Johnson White.)

Here is a graduating class from the Camp Anza cook and baker school. From left to right are (first row) Privates Claude Spencer, Henry Oster, Robert Lockwood, Claude Hickey, and Ralph Trober; (second row) Privates Sherman Branton, Arthur Hitchcock, Robert Kirkland, William Howren, Alfred Thornton, Franklin Spidle, and William Hortman; (third row) Privates Louis Freedman, Henry Long, Charles Flanders, Clay Kyte, Herbert Kent, Ray Hood, Roy Saterfield, and Lewis Goad. (Courtesy NARA.)

This is an interior view of the Camp Anza Post Office. It was located next to the camp headquarters. The building is now used as apartments on Philbin Avenue. (Courtesy NARA.)

The Western Union office was located on what is today Cypress Avenue near Challen Street. (Courtesy NARA.)

MAJOR JOHNSON BACK AT DESK MONDAY

ANZA ZIP

GRACE McDONALD ADDED TO "IN THE GROOVE"

Camp Anza had a weekly newspaper called the *Anza Zip*. The phrase "Zip a lip" was used often during World War II and appeared on several Camp Anza items. The phrase referred to not talking about military information with strangers, as did the phrase "loose lips sink ships." Camp Anza adopted the phrase. The camp's athletic teams used the name Camp Anza Zips. Each issue covered the latest news about the camp and its social life. There were also national sports reports and world news. Shown above is the banner for the camp newspaper used until a new banner was created in September 1944. Below is Sgt. George Repp, one of the editors of the *Anza Zip*. (Banner courtesy Riverside Public Library; photograph courtesy NARA.)

Chaplain Jasper Havens, at right, came to Camp Anza in October 1942. He penned a weekly column in the *Anza Zip* called "The Chaplain Speaks." One of his columns appears below. Chaplain Havens was described as a nice man who was well liked by those who met him. (Courtesy Riverside Public Library.)

Chaplain Jasper C. Havens

On Guadalcanal, we are told, the chief of a Polynesian tribe posted the following announcement on a mess-hall bulletin board:

"American soldiers are requested to please be a little more careful in their choice of language, particularly when natives are assisting them in their unloading of ships, trucks, and in erecting abodes. American missionaries spent many years among us and taught us the words we should not use. Every day, however, American soldiers use those words and the good work your missionaries did is being undermined by your careless profanity."

What a rebuke for representatives of "Christian" America!

The Wolf by Sansone

Copyright 1944 by Leonard Sansone, distributed by Camp Newspaper Service.

"—oh, let's get out of here! I don't understand
a word of French!"

After receiving spiritual guidance from Chaplain Havens, *Anza Zip* readers often turned to enjoy the antics of "The Wolf" (above), a weekly cartoon drawn by Sgt. Leonard Sansone. His cartoon was enjoyed in camps around the world. "Wolf" was a term used in the 1940s for a man who is always after a woman. A similar iconic character was created by Tex Avery for the popular MGM "Droopy" cartoons of the time. After the war, "The Wolf" cartoons were assembled and sold as a collection in book form. Below is another popular strip, "Male Call," drawn by "Terry and the Pirates" artist Milton Caniff. "Male Call" featured femme fatales who were always one step ahead of a poor infatuated GI. The implication was that the woman of your dreams may be a spy, so beware! (Courtesy Riverside Public Library.)

Another popular feature of the *Anza Zip* was the weekly pin-up girl. (Courtesy Riverside Public Library.)

She's Composed . . . Are You!

WE REALLY don't have any particular reason for running this bit of photography by Bruno of Hollywood except for the attractive earings Lois de Fee is sporting. They go well with her 6 feet four inches frame, don't you think?—Ed.

. . . . That whirlwind hustling
to town at 1700 these days is S
"Geronimo" Zink—his gal's vi
ing . . . . What gives with Ju
Petiit—every time she delivers
it arrives half melted . . .
Orchids to Capt. Gatlin and
staff: They put on a swell feed
any hour of the night for visitie
shows . . . . All of her friends wi
Angie Latina a speedy recovery
she's in the hospital at Camp Ha
with a fractured pelvic.

YOU'RE LOOKING at
Jessica Rogers who is re-
ported to possess the most
beautiful eyes in show
business. Do you agree?

Here is another pin-up from the *Anza Zip*. (Courtesy Riverside Public Library.)

The Camp Anza fire station, firefighting rigs, and staff are shown here. This fire station served as the Arlanza fire station long after World War II. The camp fire station was located on the southwest corner of Cypress Avenue and Challen Street. Today the location is used as a community garden. The current Arlanza fire station is located further west on Cypress. (Courtesy NARA.)

The Camp Anza Military Police (MP) unit is shown astride their motorcycles. From left to right are T5g. Joseph Cornell, Pfc. James French, Pfc. Oakley Hanna, T5g. Harold Goldman, and Cpl. Joseph Bauer. (Courtesy NARA.)

In 1944, Camp Anza opened the largest military laundry in the west. It served eight other camps from as far away as Las Vegas. Here a civilian employee is seen operating one of the giant-capacity washing machines. After the war, the laundry building became the western headquarters of the Burpee Seed Company. The building still stands on the southwest corner of Arlington and Rutland Avenues. (Courtesy NARA.)

After washing and drying, uniforms were pressed on large clothing presses, as shown by this civilian laundry worker. Capt. Herbert Schemme was the officer in charge of the laundry. (Courtesy NARA.)

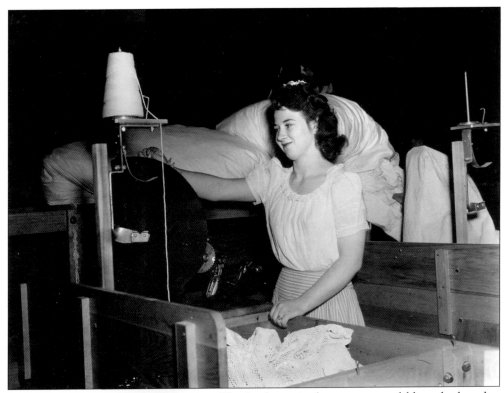

The final step in the process was folding the laundry. Finished laundry was then placed in large wooden bins on wheels. The laundry handled 1.5 million pieces each month and employed 400 workers. (Courtesy NARA.)

This raven-haired beauty is Riverside resident Lina Hernandez. She answered a newspaper advertisement announcing that civilian employees were needed for several openings at the new camp laundry. Lima's brother-in-law, Pvt. Clarence Martinez, from Casablanca was killed in action in New Guinea during WWII. (Courtesy Lina Martinez.)

Camp Anza's civilian laundry superintendent, Franklin Still, is pictured beside his employee suggestion award-winning creation; the portable press finishing bin. It was determined that his creation saved the laundry $1,200 per month in time and labor. He received $250 from Colonel Johnson for his idea. (Courtesy NARA.)

After the surrender of Italy, Italian POWs who took an oath were formed into Italian Service Units (ISUs) and moved to various camps around the United States. One ISU was sent to Camp Anza. They were housed in the Arlington Reception Center. Here the ISU is seen marching on the Camp Anza parade ground. (Courtesy NARA.)

The ISU members were issued uniforms identical to U.S. soldiers and were allowed to work in various jobs around the camp, including the mess halls and laundry. The distinctive feature of their uniform was a large green shoulder patch on which "Italy" was embroidered. They were allowed to leave camp in the company of an American officer. Here members of the ISU await a Christmas celebration. (Courtesy NARA.)

Tony and Phyllis Santamatos were married just after the war ended. Tony met Phyllis when he and other ISU members would leave camp and go her home to eat her mother's excellent Italian cooking. They built a home just north of the former Camp Anza property in the late 1940s. Tony was well known throughout the Arlanza neighborhood. He worked as a welder for Macco in Colton. (Courtesy Phyllis Santamatos.)

Civilian employees with three years of service were honored with a small ceremony attended by Colonel Sarles. From left to right are: (first row) Dorothy Starnes, Roberta Guy, and Thelma Null; (second row) Betty Kunnich, Elsie Randall, director of civilian personnel Houston Speer, Kathleen Cook, and Marion Rogers. Dorothy Starnes was one of the first civilian employees at Camp Anza, starting in October 1942. She was the leading hitter on the ladies softball team. (Courtesy NARA.)

Pictured here are military veterans who came to work at Camp Anza. From left to right are Arthur Arce, Manual Gomez, Henry Basinger, David Castro, Lyle Kennedy, Mildred Cuneo, Dana Brown, Herschel Morgan, Felix Gomez, and Cruiz Bonilla. Mildred Cuneo was a WAVE, and Cruiz Bonilla served in the U.S. Navy. All other men pictured served in the U.S. Army. (Courtesy NARA.)

Standing on the stage in the Camp Anza theater, this group comprised the advisory board for employee relations. They made suggestions and assisted in handling disputes. (Courtesy NARA.)

War bond drives were conducted frequently across the United States to fund the war effort. Camp Anza did its part by conducting its own bond drives. These lovely young ladies are signing up GIs for bond purchases. The Mounds candy bars were further incentive to visit the bond drive office. (Courtesy NARA.)

War bond officer Lt. Elaine Van Horn is seen selling war bonds to patrolmen Walter Bunyard, left, and George Murifield. Bunyard bought $4,000 worth of bonds and Murifield $1,000—both hefty sums in the 1940s. (Courtesy NARA.)

The Camp Anza band performs in front of the Camp Anza headquarters during a war bond rally. On the left side of the image, the camp chapel can be seen. Both the headquarters building and chapel still stand in the Arlanza neighborhood today. (Courtesy NARA.)

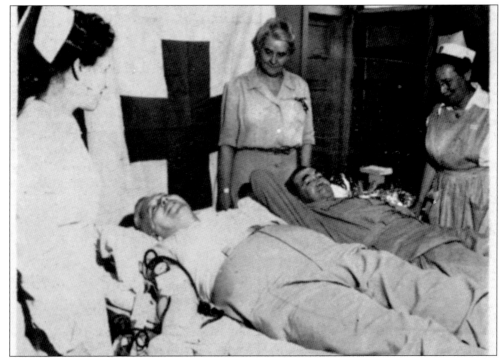

Blood was a constant and critical need for the Camp Anza Station Hospital. Colonel Sarles (left) and Col. Earl Wood, commanding officer of the station hospital (right), set the example by donating. (Courtesy Riverside Public Library.)

Awards were given for employee suggestions to improve operations at Camp Anza. This provided a sense of being listened to for the civilian employees of the camp. Gordon Zanis shows off his suggestion for a sign to warn of the firehouse door danger. (Courtesy NARA.)

Here is an interior view of one of the camp barbershops. (Courtesy NARA.)

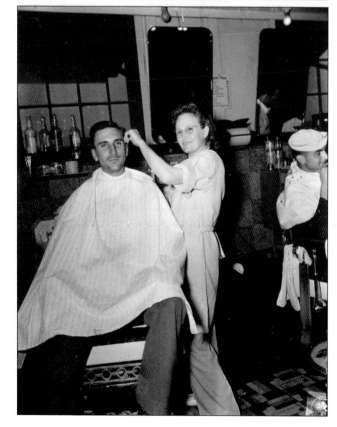

The only female barber in camp was Riverside resident Thelma Nash, seen at right cutting the hair of T5g. Henry Garsva. (Courtesy NARA.)

Here is an interior view of the main camp PX looking toward the soda fountain area. After the war, this building was used as a roller-skating rink for a time. (Courtesy NARA.)

The shopping area of the PX can be seen in this view. Toiletries, magazines, candy, and tobacco products were available for sale. (Courtesy NARA.)

A large service club was built on the east end of Camp Anza facing today's Montgomery Street, between Cypress Avenue and Philbin Avenue. It was a comfortable place to relax. The furniture could be moved, and this space was used for weekly dances for enlisted men. There was a soda fountain and barbershop in the service club. The service club was used as a school after the war. (Courtesy Frank Holznagle and Riverside Metropolitan Museum.)

There was a library upstairs in the service club. The Riverside Public Library assisted in assembling books for the Camp Anza library. (Courtesy Frank Holznagle and Riverside Metropolitan Museum.)

Billiards was available in the service club. The service club provided a place for GIs to socialize away from the cramped quarters in the barracks. (Courtesy NARA.)

Soldiers could listen to the radio in the service club. (Courtesy NARA.)

Here is an interior view of the Officer's Club at Christmas. It looked very similar inside to the enlisted men's service club. Dances were hosted for officers here. The building served as the Moose lodge for many years after the war. The building still stands on Picker Street near Philbin Avenue. It is one of very few significant Camp Anza buildings remaining in the neighborhood. (Courtesy NARA.)

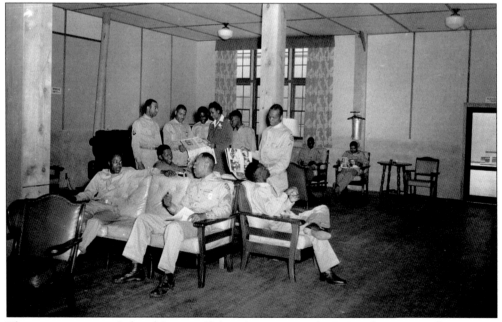

There was a separate Colored Service Club at Camp Anza. The U.S. military was still segregated during World War II. After the war, President Truman eliminated segregation in the military. Soldiers are seen here visiting with the club hostess. (Courtesy NARA.)

ISU member Federico Ferrari shows his artwork to Lt. Kenneth Buckridge, manager of the Camp Anza theater. The patch worn by Italian POWs is visible on his uniform. Ferrari painted many portraits in camp during the war, including one of the son of Col. James K. Herbert, commanding officer of the LAPE. (Courtesy NARA.)

Federico Ferrari is shown working on a painting for the Officer's Club, which had a lounge area with a tropical motif. (Courtesy NARA.)

The murals on the walls of the Officer's Club lounge were painted by Federico Ferrari. He also painted the freestanding painting at the back of the photograph. Ferrari's art creates a tropical ambience in the lounge. (Courtesy NARA.)

This dramatic Transportation Corps mural was painted in the Officer's Club by Federico Ferrari. It shows the Transportation Corps moving cargo by land, sea, and air. It was a large mural, measuring 12 feet by 30 feet. (Courtesy the Herbert family.)

In the image above, among this group of station complement officers, is Lt. Fred Woodard. He is standing in the back row, third from the right. The dashing officer caught the eye of Camp Anza civilian employee Louise Simmons. The couple was married on October 24, 1943, in the Camp Anza chapel in a service performed by Chaplain Jasper C. Havens. The newlyweds are shown at left. After the war, Fred built a home just west of the Camp Anza property. Building materials were in short supply after the war, so Fred got permission to use some windows from Camp Anza buildings, slated for demolition, for use in his new home. (Above, courtesy NARA; below, courtesy Fred and Louise Woodard.)

At the same time that Lieutenant Woodard caught Louise's eye, fellow civilian employee and Louise's best friend, Muriel Grace Mathews, saw the young officer with Lieutenant Woodard and was immediately smitten with Lt. Richard King. Later in the war, Muriel joined the WAVES and married Tony, as Lieutenant King was called. In the photograph above, Muriel is on the right, with fellow WAVES, showing the winning smile that beguiled many a soldier at Camp Anza. She played on the Camp Anza ladies softball team (see page 85). Lieutenant King is shown in the photograph at right. (Courtesy Pam Skumawitz.)

yours always
Tony

Fred and Louise are seen here with their first-born child, Warren. They raised their family in Arlanza in the years after the war. Their daughter Bonnie attended Wells Intermediate School and Norte Vista High School with the author. (Courtesy Pam Skumawitz.)

The Woodards and the Kings are seen in a lighter moment during the war while posing for a novelty photograph at a seaside amusement park. The couples continued their friendship long after the war. (Courtesy Pam Skumawitz.)

Employees of the motor pool are seen washing military vehicles. The addition of female drivers in the motor pool proved to be quite popular. (Courtesy NARA.)

One of the drivers at Camp Anza was Dede Webber, shown here with her husband Warren. She was a beauty queen contest winner at nearby March Field during the war. The couple lived and raised their daughter, Linda, and son, Dennis, in nearby La Sierra. Dennis attended Norte Vista High School with the author. Warren worked for many years at Rohr Aircraft, which moved to the Camp Anza property after the war. (Courtesy Dennis Webber.)

One motor pool employee, Judy Pettit, went on to become a part of the entertainment staff at Camp Anza. Her singing was very much enjoyed by camp audiences. She met and married Howard Randall in the Camp Anza chapel. Randall was a member of the Camp Anza band. Judy Pettit was the half sister of Riverside's *Press Enterprise* history columnist, Hal Durian. (Courtesy Riverside Public Library.)

Howard Randall is in the front row, third from the right, shown here playing in the dance band led by Nick Buono. Private Buono was an excellent trumpet player who played in Harry James's bands for several decades, appearing on several of his albums. He also appeared in several movies as part of Harry James's band. (Courtesy NARA.)

Here is a scene from *Springtime in the Rockies*, a movie featuring Harry James and his orchestra. Nick Buono can be seen in the far back row playing trumpet, second from the right. (Courtesy Frank Teurlay.)

Another popular Camp Anza dance band was headed by Vernon Kline. He is seen here standing on the left, saxophone in hand. Kline was a studio musician at MGM before the war. The Buono and Kline dance bands performed at dances frequently during the war. (Courtesy NARA.)

A popular song during World War II was the Andrews Sisters' hit *Boogie Woogie Bugle Boy*. Camp Anza had its very own boogie woogie bugle boy in Nick Buono, shown here "blowing eight to the bar in boogie rhythm." The occasion was a formal Halloween dance in October 1944. (Courtesy NARA.)

Patsy Parker sings at the Halloween formal. She sang in the Harry James band and was the wife of Nick Buono. (Courtesy NARA.)

This formal was reported to be the finest dance held at the camp. In these high-perspective views, the crowded dance floor is seen in the photograph above. Local young ladies from Arlington and Riverside were invited to the dances at the service club to provide dance partners for the GIs. Below, Patsy Buono is seen singing in front of the band. A sumptuous buffet was provided for the attendees. (Courtesy NARA.)

Drummer Rod Rodriguez had a winning smile and was voted the best-looking GI in Camp Anza by the female employees of the camp. Rodriguez played in the dance bands and the marching band. He lived in Pasadena before the war and had acquired a collection of over 3,000 phonograph records. (Courtesy NARA.)

The Camp Anza marching band greeted arriving troop trains and provided a musical send-off for departing troops. The band also performed concerts for the public in Arlington Park and Fairmount Park in Riverside. At the end of the war, the Camp Anza band had the honor of marching in a victory parade in Los Angeles. (Courtesy the Herbert family.)

This group of entertainers performed throughout the camp in the theaters, service clubs, and the station hospital. The singer at the microphone is Pfc. Joe Tobin. The dancer is Pfc. Sammy Greene, who was very popular. The accordion player is Pfc. Julio Guilietti, who won a music competition as the best accordion player in the 9th Service Command. The man playing guitar is Sgt. Arthur Todd, director of entertainment. On piano is his wife, Dotty. They recorded the hit tune *Chanson d'Amour* in 1958, which reached number six on the charts. They had their own radio show after the war and later appeared in Las Vegas and on television on such programs as the Steve Allen Show and American Bandstand. At right is the sheet music for *Chanson d'Amour*, featuring Art and Dotty. (Above, courtesy NARA; below, courtesy Frank Teurlay.)

Shown above is Lt. Kenneth Buckridge in his office. Lieutenant Buckridge, a native of New York, was manager of Theater One at Camp Anza. He was able to procure first-run Hollywood movies to show in camp before they were released nationally. (Courtesy NARA.)

Here are Pvt. Larry Shields (left) and Cpl. Bob Elder in the radio control room in Theater One. Bob Elder owned the nearby Arlington Theater and arranged with Lieutenant Buckridge to take first-run movies from camp to show at his theater. Therefore Arlington residents were seeing new Hollywood movies before the rest of the country. (Courtesy NARA.)

This image shows a clear view of the seating and stage in Theater One. A band and chorus are seen rehearsing for a Christmas show. (Courtesy NARA.)

Pvt. Frank "Bud" Holznagle was stationed at Camp Anza and knew Bob Elder and Lieutenant Buckridge. He recalls Art and Dotty Todd performing throughout camp and leading the audience in a song very similar to their hit nearly 15 years later, *Chanson d'Amour*. His favorite was the emcee of camps shows, Sol Feltzen. He could do a quick-paced scat, similar to Danny Kaye, that delighted audiences. (Courtesy Frank Holznagle.)

An outdoor theater was built behind the gymnasium on the east end of camp near Van Buren Boulevard. It was christened by Lucille Ball, and Tommy Dorsey's was the first big band to grace its stage. It was here that Lena Horne sang *Stormy Weather* and Harpo Marx, noted for his pantomime, spoke to the GIs at Camp Anza, a rare, documented account of him speaking in public. (Courtesy NARA.)

Dancing girls were a regular part of the travelling shows that came to army camps throughout the world. In this photograph, happy GIs are spending a few moments with the brightly costumed chorus girls of the famous MGM musicals of the 1940s. (Courtesy NARA.)

Orson Welles is shown at right performing a sleight of hand with a member of the Camp Anza audience. Below is a view of the audience from above the stage. Halfway back, on a row of benches, Colonel Herbert and Colonel Sarles are seated. The story goes that a Hollywood performer, perhaps Jimmy Durante, once came on stage and saw officers occupying the front rows with the enlisted men in the rear. The performer said something like, "I'm here to perform for the GIs, all you officers to the rear or I don't go on." He left the stage and did not return until the seating was reversed. This may be why we see the commanding officers seated back from the stage in this photograph. (Courtesy NARA.)

In March 1945, Bob Hope brought his popular weekly *Pepsodent Radio Program* to Theater One at Camp Anza. The show was broadcast nationally on NBC radio. Here Bob Hope is seen during the broadcast performing with guest Shirley Temple. Later in the show, Jerry Colonna came out for a couple of skits. In one, he warns GIs "stay away from strange women at the Mission Inn, that's my territory." (Courtesy the Herbert family.)

Popular singer and veteran of Bob Hope's USO shows, Frances Langford made an appearance on the program. She was greeted with thunderous applause that drowned out the opening notes of her song as she appeared on stage in a stunning gown that was well appreciated by the GI crowd. She sang an emotional song that implored the troops to take care and return home safely. (Courtesy the Herbert family.)

After the show, Colonel Sarles hosted Bob Hope in the Officer's Club. They are seen here admiring the painting and murals of Federico Ferrari in the tropical lounge area. The broadcast marked Hope's fourth anniversary of performing shows for troops and was acknowledged by the U.S. Department of War at the end of the program. His very first troop show was performed at nearby March Field. (Courtesy NARA.)

In October 1945, the Bob Hope program returned for another national broadcast of his popular weekly radio program. He is seen here on stage with Frances Langford signing autographs for the GIs after the show. (Courtesy NARA.)

Kay Kyser brought his popular *College of Musical Knowledge* radio program to Camp Anza in April 1945. The show was broadcast nationally from Theater One. (Courtesy NARA.)

Local camp talent was often used to supplement the larger shows that came to camp. Here is an informal dance with a small band and singers. The lady seated to the left looks a bit forlorn at not having a dance partner. (Courtesy NARA.)

Cpl. Alfred Aguirre served in the Pacific and was awarded the Bronze Star. He was stationed for a time at Camp Anza. In his memoirs, he mentions seeing Desi Arnaz at Camp Anza and sharing barracks with the actor Sabu, star of such movies as *The Jungle Book* (1942) and *Arabian Nights* (1942). Aguirre's nephew, Mars Macias (page 123), established Mars Barber Shop in a former Camp Anza building. (Courtesy Mars Macias.)

In his autobiography, Desi Arnaz tells of his time at the Arlington Reception Center. He was ready to ship out to bombardier school but was derailed when he injured his knee in a pick-up baseball game. Unable to meet the physical requirements, Private Arnaz was assigned to provide training and entertainment at Camp Anza. His wife, Lucille Ball, was often seen visiting him at Camp Anza. (Courtesy Frank Teurlay.)

In addition to entertainment, Camp Anza offered a wide array of athletic venues and activities. Pictured at left is the interior of the camp gymnasium. In back of this building the boxer, Joe Louis, and the top female athlete of her time, Babe Didrikson Zaharias, put on sporting exhibitions for the enjoyment of the troops. This building was located on the west side of Challen Street behind the playground of Arlanza Elementary School. (Courtesy NARA.)

Shown here is the Camp Anza basketball team, which competed in the Riverside YMCA league. From left to right are Technician Fifth Grade Zimmerman, Technician Fourth Grade Brown, Sergeant Eisen, Corporal Neely, Lieutenant Weaver (coach), Private Canino, Sergeant Anderson, Corporal Hillo, and Technician Fourth Grade Stepanski. While the army was segregated, the Camp Anza sports teams were not, as evidenced by the presence of Corporal Neely. Corporal Neely also played on the Camp Anza softball team. (Courtesy NARA.)

Here is a team photograph of the champion Anza Zips softball team. The Zips won the 9th Service Command softball championship for Camp Anza two years running, in 1944 and 1945. Star pitcher Bob Beslack threw many no-hit, no-run games on the road to the titles. He is pictured standing and smiling in the back row, third from the right. (Courtesy NARA.)

Bob Beslack shows his form while Zips coach Lieutenant Feld and outfielder Ray Lee look on. Beslack also served in the Camp Anza color guard for parade events. After the war, Beslack continued his career as a softball pitcher and worked for 30 years in the auto industry in Detroit. (Courtesy NARA.)

Catcher Hank Ribacchi crouches behind the plate during a Zips practice. Ribacchi played professional baseball at the AAA level. In the background is the back of the Camp Anza fire station. This photograph was taken on a spot that today would be the northeast portion of the Arlanza Elementary School playground. (Courtesy NARA.)

This photograph of the Zips practice shows the back of the Camp Anza gymnasium in the background. Bob Beslack is seen backing up the play at second base. (Courtesy NARA.)

Camp Anza also had a ladies softball team with a winning record. From left to right are (first row) Cherry Correll, Dorothy Minor, Muriel Mathews (page 65), and June Horsley; (second row) Dorothy Starnes, Earline Cullins, coach Fred Matteson, Dorothea Swartz, and Florence Presley. (Courtesy NARA.)

There was a bowling alley in a recreation building on the east end of Camp Anza near the service club. Bowling was extremely popular, and there were several leagues operating at any given time. (Courtesy NARA.)

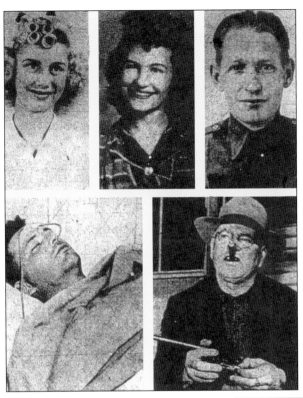

In March 1944, Lt. Beaufort Swancutt shot and killed his mistress and her friend in the Officer's Club. He left camp and was confronted by two Riverside police officers on Magnolia in Arlington. He was shot by officer Ernest Cole after fatally shooting officer Arthur Simpson. Pictured at left are those involved. In the upper left is Lourdine Livermore, a friend of Swancutt's mistress, Dorothy Douglas (center). In the lower left, Lieutenant Swancutt is seen lying in the Camp Anza Station Hospital. The officer above is Arthur Simpson. Officer Ernest Cole, who wounded Swancutt, is in the lower right showing his service revolver used in the gun battle. Below, officer Cole stands at attention. The Riverside Police Department's Award for Valor is named for officer Cole. (Left, courtesy Long Beach Library; below, courtesy Riverside Police Department.)

Four

COMING HOME

While Camp Anza staged nearly a quarter of a million troops on their way to the Pacific during the war, it welcomed home nearly twice that many as the war ended. Col. Thomas Meyer was named the commanding officer of the Debarkation Command Group. It was his task to organize an efficient process for inactivating army units and processing the GIs through the camp within 24 to 48 hours. He personally greeted each unit coming into Camp Anza after serving in the Pacific. From Camp Anza, troops took a train to their final discharge point.

Camp Anza had the honor of welcoming home two highly decorated infantry divisions whose exploits were well known to Americans during the war. The 38th Infantry Division fought valiantly in the Philippines and earned distinction by retaking the Bataan Peninsula from the Japanese. In 1942, several thousand American and Philippine soldiers and civilians were forcibly marched up the Bataan Peninsula to a concentration camp. Without provisions and due to harsh treatment at the hands of their captors, some 6,000 to 11,000 died. The atrocity horrified the American public and made heroes of the men who retook the region three years later. The 38th officially earned the title "Avengers of Bataan" for this accomplishment. The 96th Infantry Division, known as the "Deadeyes," fought with distinction in the last and bloodiest land battle of World War II, Okinawa. Camp Anza was honored to be the first location to officially welcome home these victorious divisions.

The story of their welcome home is seen in this chapter through the eyes of the men of the 38th and 96th. Once in Camp Anza, war-weary GIs were given their first taste of home. A steak dinner, a trip to the soda fountain, a new uniform, some music on the jukebox, and a phone call home were all amenities gladly provided for the troops coming home through Camp Anza.

Sgt. Wilson Brummett served with the 38th Infantry Division as part of the 150th Field Artillery. He is pictured here with a Filipino boy he befriended during the campaign in the Philippines. His niece, Ruby Gwin, wrote a self-published account of her uncle's service with the 38th. In it, he talks about coming to Camp Anza and enjoying clean white linen and blankets. (Courtesy Ruby Gwin.)

The 38th shows pride in their accomplishment with a sign announcing that Bataan is safe to enter. (Courtesy Frank Teurlay.)

WELCOME HOME
"AVENGERS OF BATAAN"

First "Cyclones" Will Arrive This Weekend

Volume 3   Camp Anza, Arlington, California, October 25, 1945   Number 36

The first increment of the famous 38th "Cyclone" Infantry Division which will be disbanded and put on the inactive list of the Army at Camp Anza will arrive here on Saturday.

The advance party will consist of approximately 200 officers and 4,300 enlisted men who will dock sometime Saturday at the Los Angeles Port of Embarkation at Wilmington aboard the USS Uruguay.

They will represent elements of the 149th Infantry Regiment, Headquarters and Headquarters Battery of the Division Artillery, 38th Signal Company, 38th Cavalry Reconnaisance Troop, and an Anti-Tank Company of the 152d Infantry Regiment.

16,000 In All

The first arrivals will be followed by various units of the division until the entire strength, estimated at 16,000 men, is processed at this station and sent on to separation centers throughout the country for disposition. Many of the 38th men have seen action in other outfits.

On Monday 1459 additional Cyclone boys are scheduled to dock at LAPE. Wednesday will find 5577 more officers and enlisted men of the division in camp.

Here 24 Hours

2000 Vets Processed by New System

The Debarkation Command Group's new method of processing debarkees went into practice last weekend as more than 2,000 overseas veterans were received here.

Processing Team Number One, of which Lt. Col. Winston Butscher is chief, took charge of 931 enlisted men and 68 officers who docked at the LAPE Saturday on the USS Takonis Bay.

On Sunday trains pulled into camp with 1284 EM and 54 officers aboard. These groups were taken in hand by Processing Team Number Two headed by Lt. Col. Charles E. Packard.

A few hours after Sunday's arrivals had been received and billeted the GIs who had come to camp on Saturday were put aboard trains headed east for

38th Division Veterans Of Bataan and Manila

The famed 38th "Cyclone" Infantry Division will be recorded in military history as the "Avengers of Bataan."

The division went overseas in December, 1943. The battle action of the 38th was centered in Bataan and the region northeast of Manila beginning December 7, 1944, just three years after Pearl Harbor.

Spearheading the drive which annihilated Japanese forces on Bataan, in the battle that liberated Luzon, is an achievement of which men of the 38th are justly proud.

The division got its first taste of battle when the 149th Infantry Regiment was sent into Leyte, P. I., to make its now famous Subic Bay landing on Bataan Peninsula on January 29, 1945.

Division troops poured in for 16 days of fierce action to smash through an intricate maze of Japanese fortifications at Zig-Zag Pass, key defense to the rapid reduction of Bataan Peninsula.

While one division regimental combat team made an amphibious landing on Mariveles, on the tip of the Peninsula, another force

ganized from the 38th division artillery, struck north and west of Zig-Zag Pass against powerful Jap defenses in the Zambales mountain ranges, while the third regimental combat team was charged with the reduction of enemy defenses on the remaining three islands—Cabello, Fort Drum and Carabao—guarding the entrance to Manila Bay. Later sent to the Marakina water shed, the Cyclone boys worked in May

AT EASE!
CYCLONES

Welcome to Camp Anza, and to your home soil. Congratulations on the marvelous job you have done overseas. Camp Anza has but one mission, and that is to get you on your way home as quickly as possible. To do this, we must have your whole hearted and constant cooperation.

This is your special edition of the Anza Zip. Read it carefully, as it contains much matter of interest to you.

On your way to Camp Anza

The USS *Uruguay* steams toward the Los Angeles Port of Embarkation. As far out as Catalina Island, a blimp appeared in the sky with loudspeakers playing Dinah Shore's rendition of "It's Been a Long, Long Time." The men of the 38th knew it would not be long before they would be back on U.S. soil. (Courtesy the Herbert family.)

The *Anza Zip* ran a special banner headline announcing the anticipated arrival of the famed 38th Infantry Division at Camp Anza. (Courtesy Riverside Public Library.)

The ladies pictured above made up the stenographer pool at the LAPE. In the back row, second from the right, is 19-year-old Ruby Fanning. Her first job was at the LAPE. She recalls taking advantage of a standing offer to get a half-day off if the ladies would agree to go out on a small greeter boat and wave to the returning GIs as their ship came into the harbor. Below, the greeter boat, which was christened the *Snafu Maru*, comes in close to a troop ship. No doubt Ruby is there on deck waving to the GIs. After the war, Ruby married Carl Jordan and lived for many years in the Arlanza area, where she and her family befriended the author. Carl worked at Rohr in the 1950s. (Above, courtesy Ruby Jordan; below courtesy the Herbert family.)

Gen. Frederick A. Irving, commander of the 38th, addresses his division from the deck of the *Snafu Maru*. He commended them for their service and wished them well as they returned to civilian life. (Courtesy the Herbert family.)

Popular radio singer Connie Haynes was on the pier to sing to the GIs aboard ship as it pulled into its berth. (Courtesy the Herbert family.)

Members of the 38th leave the ship while others on deck await their turn. (Courtesy the Herbert family.)

Soldiers carry their gear through the warehouse and out to the train. (Courtesy the Herbert family.)

The Avengers of Bataan board the train for Camp Anza. (Courtesy the Herbert family.)

Upon arrival at Camp Anza, GIs leave the train with their duffle bags. (Courtesy the Herbert family.)

The soldiers line up to await their barracks assignments and to learn what they will be doing while in camp. (Courtesy the Herbert family.)

Col. Thomas Meyer greets the 38th Infantry Division in front of a specially painted welcome sign. (Courtesy NARA.)

Colonel Meyer conducts an orientation for the troops. He explains the benefits of the GI Bill and what to expect while in camp. (Courtesy NARA.)

This is the cover of a small multifold paper that opened to inform soldiers about what to expect during their time in Camp Anza. It featured a welcome-home message from newly promoted Gen. James K. Herbert. (Courtesy Frank Teurlay.)

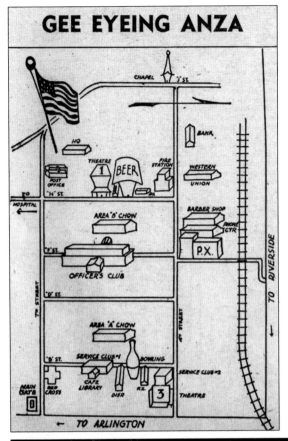

GEE EYEING ANZA

CHAPEL · "J" St.
BANK
HQ
FIRE STATION
POST OFFICE
THEATRE 1
BEER
WESTERN UNION
"H" St.
TO HOSPITAL
AREA "B" CHOW
BARBER SHOP
PHONE CTR
"F" St.
P.X.
OFFICER'S CLUB
"D" St.
7TH STREET
AREA "A" CHOW
4TH STREET
TO RIVERSIDE
"B" St.
SERVICE CLUB #1
BOWLING
SERVICE CLUB #2
MAIN GATE
RED CROSS
CAFE LIBRARY
DISP
P.X.
THEATRE 3
TO ARLINGTON

This small map was printed in the *Anza Zip* to orient the returning GIs to the camp layout and where important buildings could be found. Running the length of the map are Fourth and Seventh Streets. Today these streets are Cypress Avenue and Philbin Avenue. Note that the gymnasium has been converted into a beer garden next to Thatre One. (Courtesy Riverside Public Library.)

The 38th (below) have had a chance to clean up from their journey and head into the mess hall for a hot meal. (Courtesy the Herbert family.)

Serving trays in hand, the members of the 38th proceed through the chow line in one of the mess halls. Every soldier received a ticket for a steak dinner to be enjoyed during his stay in camp. (Courtesy the Herbert family.)

One last helping is added to this GI's tray. (Courtesy NARA.)

Members of the 38th enjoy a milk shake at one of the PX soda fountains. (Courtesy NARA.)

GIs enjoy a song at the jukebox. (Courtesy the Herbert family.)

Camp Anza built one of the largest telephone centers in the country for the express purpose of enabling the returning GIs to talk for the first time with family members. (Courtesy NARA.)

A visit to the PX was in order to get a gift for that special someone. The jewelry counter did a booming business. (Courtesy the Herbert family.)

Since they arrived in late October, GIs were issued new Class A cold-weather uniforms for the trip home. (Courtesy NARA.)

A bed with sheets was a much-welcomed luxury for the troops used to sleeping in foxholes and shipboard bunks. (Courtesy NARA.)

The 96th Infantry Division broke with tradition and voted for Marjorie Main as their favorite pin-up girl. She was famous for her portrayals of Ma in the Ma and Pa Kettle movies. Excited to have been selected, she vowed greet them when their ship came in. When they arrived, she boarded the ship and visited with the GIs after turning down an offer to have lunch with the officers. She is seen at right celebrating with the Deadeyes. She took a car to Camp Anza, arriving before their troop train. She was in the mess hall serving line to serve her Deadeyes as they arrived. After the photograph below was taken, the mess officer pulled her off chow line duty when he realized that she was giving each member of the 96th two steaks instead of one. (Courtesy Frank Teurlay.)

Having been issued new uniforms and with new patches to be sewn on, GIs turn to E. Bell and Grace Walker. The ladies offered to do simple sewing for GIs in the service club. They would also hem slacks. (Courtesy NARA.)

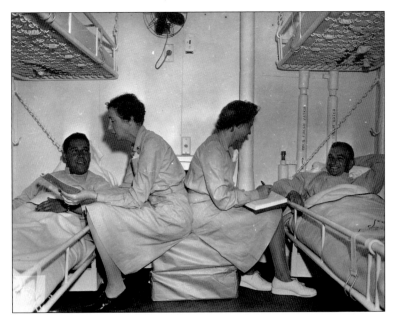

Wounded GIs also came home via Camp Anza. In this photograph, army nurses on the hospital ship *Mercy* visit with homebound GIs. The nurses assigned to the *Mercy* were trained for their mission at Camp Anza. (Courtesy NARA.)

Colonel Herbert was promoted to brigadier general in September 1945, making him the youngest general in the U.S. Army at the time. He is shown here at the LAPE with his wife, Mary Louise, and his new general's flag. (Courtesy the Herbert family.)

At Camp Anza, General Herbert awards the Legion of Merit medal to Col. Walter Johnson, the father of Camp Anza. Also pictured is Julio Guilietti, who received an award for winning the music competition for the 9th Service Command as best accordion player. (Courtesy the Herbert family.)

This street-level view shows GIs arriving at camp in December 1945. This photograph was taken on Cypress Avenue looking east from Challen Street. The PX in the distance would be near Picker Street. All of the GIs in the foreground appear relaxed, no doubt happy to be headed home. (Courtesy Frank Teurlay.)

This advertisement, placed by Rohr Aircraft Corporation in *Time* magazine in 1944, encourages businesses to consider the Pacific coast as an excellent place to do business after the war. Interestingly, the executive in the advertisement is pointing very close to a location to which Rohr would expand nearly a decade later. (Courtesy Frank Teurlay.)

Five

POST-WAR DEVELOPMENT

After World War II, the War Assets Department was responsible for selling off property no longer needed. Camp Anza was put up for sale and purchased by the Anza Realty Company. Anza Realty wanted to sell a large parcel quickly to raise cash to develop other parts of the camp property. They were successful in luring Rohr Aircraft Corporation and the Burpee Seed Company to the former army camp. Rohr bought a long narrow strip of land just south of Arlington Avenue, between Van Buren Boulevard and Rutland Avenue. Their Riverside plant was up and running by 1953. The Burpee Seed Company bought the former camp laundry building at the corner of Rutland and Arlington. Concurrently, the Riverside School District purchased 10 station hospital buildings and moved them to various schools for use as classrooms at overcrowded schools. Barracks were cut in half and sold as single-family homes throughout the former camp area. Some barracks were moved from the camp property to lots in nearby Arlington and as far away as La Sierra and Corona. The areas south of Philbin Avenue and north of Arlington Avenue were developed with newly constructed single-family homes. Schools were built to serve the new neighborhoods. The area became known as Anza Village. When mail intended for the desert town of Anza was being misrouted to Anza Village, a name change was in order. The name Arlanza was chosen.

Rohr Riverside became the headquarters for the company's Space Products Division in 1963. In Arlanza, Titan III rocket parts that would go into space were insulated and assembled. Goodrich purchased Rohr Industries in 1997 and continues as a subcontractor to Boeing, making parts for the newest jet, the 787 Dreamliner.

Present-day Arlanza has come a long way since 1942, when it was an alfalfa field. It has sent soldiers off to war and welcomed them home. Since then, it has played a vital role in man's attempt to reach for the stars. Perhaps most importantly, it has been home to generations of families who have many happy memories and a special fondness for this unique neighborhood.

This advertisement, placed by the War Assets Department, ran in several newspapers to announce the sale of the Camp Anza property and the buildings on the land. It touted the fact that roadways, water, and electricity were already in place. (Courtesy NARA.)

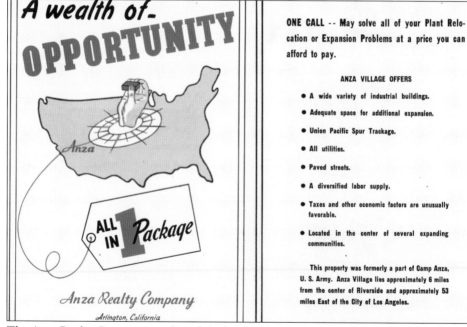

The Anza Realty Company purchased the land and prepared to sell the former camp property in parcels for development. Here is the front cover and interior page from an Anza Realty pamphlet announcing a large parcel of former Camp Anza property for sale. Rohr Corporation purchased the lot offered in this sale. Burpee Seed Company bought the former laundry building, which was also offered in this pamphlet. (Courtesy Riverside Public Library.)

The Burpee Seed Company and Rohr Aircraft Corporation were among the first and certainly the largest businesses to come to Anza Village. Burpee Seed Company was headquartered in Philadelphia, Pennsylvania. Rohr was headquartered in Chula Vista, California. (Courtesy Frank Teurlay.)

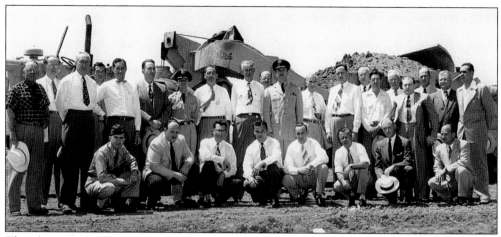

The photograph above was taken at the ground-breaking ceremony for the Rohr Riverside Plant. Fred Rohr, founder and president of Rohr Aircraft Corporation, can be seen standing in the center of the photograph. Below is an aerial view of the new plant taken on March 4, 1955. In the foreground, buildings from Girls Town can be seen. This area was part of the Arlington Reception Center during the war. In the left center of the image, Area B of Camp Anza, with the mess hall surrounded by barracks, appears little changed since the war. Above Area B, new homes can be seen under construction on the site of the station hospital. Today the street names are Rutland Avenue, Ivanhoe Avenue, and Challen Street. In the far distance, La Sierra can be seen. (Courtesy Goodrich Aerostructures.)

Arlanza Village

Estimated population, 4,000   Altitude, 740

The commercial possibilities of the area west and southwest of the city of Riverside has made this one-time agricultural region a prime location for future industrialization and commercial development.

The trade area stretches about 6½ miles to the west, 4½ miles to the east, 4 miles south and 6 miles north.

Arlanza Village now occupies land used during World War II as the Camp Anza Staging Area.

The image and caption above appeared in a c. 1953 pamphlet designed to entice people to consider moving to Riverside. Various neighborhoods were described, including this early reference to Arlanza Village. Prior to this, the neighborhood was known as Anza Village. Below is a photograph taken in 1953 on the steps of the former Camp Anza chapel after a confirmation service at the Faith Lutheran Church. Pastor August Stahnke, pictured here, is credited with coming up with the name Arlanza by combining "Arl" from Arlington Avenue and "Anza" from the former Camp Anza. However, the word Arlanza existed before 1953. There is a river in Spain called the Rio Arlanza, and a British ship christened the *Arlanza* around 1915 ran between England and South America. Others in the photograph are, from left to right, La Von Tomlinson, Ralph Schuler, and Paul Semrau. (Above, courtesy Frank Teurlay; below, courtesy the Schuler family.)

These two photographs show an officer's barracks on Picker Street purchased by the Schuler family in 1948. They were one of the first families to move into the neighborhood. These barracks were 100 feet long and 20 feet wide and were situated between Picker and Wohlstetter Streets. There was no plumbing or electricity. Each family had to arrange for theses utilities to be connected. John Schuler reports that his family had to use a neighboring Camp Anza latrine until plumbing was connected to their home. There was a lot of work ahead for families moving into the neighborhood and converting these barracks into homes. (Courtesy the Schuler family.)

In 1952, the Schulers hired a man to stucco the former barracks. He chewed tobacco as he worked and would spit the tobacco juice into the stucco mixture. He claimed that it made the stucco better. We may never know if that is true, but these photographs show the transition of the former barracks into a nice family residence. This scenario was played out many times as families transformed the former barracks into single-family homes throughout the area between Cypress Avenue and Philbin Avenue and Montgomery Street and Rutland Avenue. (Courtesy the Schuler family.)

GIRLS' TOWN CHRISTIAN SCHOOL
7911 ARLINGTON AVE., ARLINGTON, CALIF.

The Arlington Reception Center became Girls Town after the war. During the war, this location housed Italian POWs, including Tony Santamatos (page 52). Little did he know at the time that he would spend the rest of his life just a few hundred yards away. The home he and his wife Phyllis built in the late 1940s is seen in the upper left. (Courtesy Frank Teurlay.)

This advertisement shows the businesses that came to the southwest corner of Arlington Avenue and Van Buren Boulevard in the early 1960s. Little Oscar, the mascot for Oscar Mayer wieners, made an appearance here driving the famous Wienermobile and handing out Wienerwhistles. Little Oscar was really Jerry Maren, who played the Lollipop Guild Munchkin who hands a lollipop to Judy Garland in 1939's *Wizard of Oz*. (Courtesy Frank Teurlay.)

Leo and Mela Lueras bought a barracks along Cypress Avenue and converted it into Leo and Mela's Market. They were fixtures in the neighborhood for many years and were appreciated for running a tab for many customers who had a hard time making ends meet. Leo and Mela lived in the back of their market, shown above. Later Leo worked for Anza Realty and states that he was probably involved in every real estate sale in Arlanza for many years. Below, Leo (seated) and Mela are shown in their real estate office in the 1960s with candidate for city council Charles Johnson. (Courtesy Leo Lueras.)

Melvin and Gary St. George opened the Anza Service Station at 8730 Arlington Avenue in the early 1950s. Melvin and Gary are pictured at left standing on the east side of the station. A front view of the station is shown below. (Courtesy Joe St. George.)

More than 50 years later, the grandson and great-grandson of Melvin St. George are seen standing in the same location. Joe St. George now operates Howard's Rents on the same site as the Anza Service Station. Joe is pictured above (left) with his son, Richard. The author and Joe attended Norte Vista High School at the same time. (Courtesy Joe St. George.)

Here is the Rohr Corporation softball team. Carl Jordan is standing fourth from the right. Carl married Ruby Fanning (page 90) and lived in Arlanza for many years. Carl passed on his love of baseball to the youths he coached in little league and pony league. (Courtesy Frank Teurlay.)

Mickey Mouse and Donald Duck visit the author's mother, Clara Teurlay, as part of a promotion to publicize Rohr Night at Disneyland. Each year in March, Rohr Corporation reserved Disneyland for the exclusive use of its employees for an entire evening. In the days of ticket books at Disneyland, the annual Rohr Night event allowed guests unlimited use of the attractions without the need for tickets. (Courtesy Clara Teurlay.)

This 1963 aerial view shows the Hall of Giants, a seven-story building constructed to support the making of high-quality space components. The Rohr Space Products Division was headquartered at the Riverside plant. The upper right portion of the photograph shows the homes built on the north side of Arlington Avenue after the war. (Courtesy Goodrich Aerostructures.)

The advertisement (right) shows the interior of the Hall of Giants building. At the top of the advertisement, a rocket engine case insulated at Rohr Riverside can be seen. Below, the cover of a *Rohr Magazine* issue from 1963 shows a Titan III rocket for which the thrust nozzles were insulated at the Riverside plant in Arlanza. (Courtesy Frank Teurlay.)

156" rocket engine case insulated by Rohr for Lockheed Propulsion Company in 12 days.

We have the facility for major missile components

This new, highly-specialized manufacturing facility is in operation now at the Space Products Division of Rohr Corporation. Here you will find concentrated management control, advanced technology, and efficient organization backed up by broad associated skills, facilities, experience and financial support of the parent company. This unique manufacturing complex has been assembled to fill a need for customers involved in advanced space programs . . . by producing high quality **space components faster** and at **lower cost**. Technical competence and eagerness to accept challenge typify the carefully selected personnel now staffing this new Division. Unusual capabilities are available based on important experience with such products as **insulation for solid propellant rocket motor cases, nozzles for solid propellant rocket motors** including the ablative tape wrapped liner, ablative nozzle extensions for liquid propellant engines, filament wound glass fiber structures, and a variety of fiber-glass laminate products for space vehicles, helicopters, etc. For specific information, write Marketing Manager, Dept. 75, Space Products Division, Rohr Corporation, Riverside, California.

SPACE
PRODUCTS
DIVISION

ROHR CORPORATION

ROHR MAGAZINE Summer—1963

Titan III-C Space Launch Vehicle

Soon after World War II, General Herbert retired from the army. He went on to serve as an executive of the Roma Winery in Fresno, California. He also served two terms as president of the Fresno Chamber of Commerce. He is seen in the photograph above, with his wife Mary Louise (page 103), at a reunion event marking the 50th anniversary of his graduation from West Point as part of the class of 1930. Upon his passing in 1990, his estate had a provision for a generous $3-million donation to West Point. In his honor, the Alumni Center at West Point is named Herbert Hall, shown below. (Courtesy the Herbert family.)

Federico Ferrari (page 62) married his American sweetheart, Irene Dalla Rosa, and returned to live in the United States. He became a painter at the Pacific Outdoor billboard company in Los Angeles. Above, he is shown painting a billboard. Federico Ferrari had a great talent for realistic painting on a large scale. His billboards had an almost photographic clarity, as seen in his billboard painting below featuring the singer/actress Carol Lawrence. (Courtesy the Ferrari family.)

Federico Ferrari went on to become an executive at the Pacific Outdoor company. He appears quite distinguished in this company portrait. (Courtesy the Ferrari family.)

Fred Woodard joined the Riverside Fire Department after the war. He served for a time at the Arlanza Fire Station. Fred went on to become a battalion chief. He retired from the department in 1977 after 29 years of service. (Courtesy Fred and Louise Woodard.)

Fred and Louise Woodard (page 64) returned, for the first time in nearly 65 years, to the former Camp Anza chapel, where they were married by Chaplain Havens. The Woodards still live near the former Camp Anza property in the house Fred built in the late 1940s. Louise worked for the Alvord School District for many years. (Courtesy Frank Teurlay.)

The former Camp Anza chapel still stands on Chapel Street in Arlanza. (Courtesy Frank Teurlay.)

The former Camp Anza headquarters is now the Irrometer Company on Philbin Avenue. William Hawkins bought the property in 1948 and set up his ceramics business there. In the early 1950s, T. W. Prosser asked Hawkins to make the ceramic parts needed for a device that would measure the moisture in the soil. Hence the Irrometer Company was created. (Courtesy Frank Teurlay.)

The Officer's Club still stands on Picker Street near Philbin Avenue. The Moose lodge used the building for many years. Along with the camp headquarters, it is one of a very few significant Camp Anza buildings that remain in the neighborhood. It is hoped that this building will someday be given landmark status in honor of the World War II veterans who passed through or served at Camp Anza. (Courtesy Frank Teurlay.)

Mars Macias is seen here in the doorway of his barbershop at 8739 Cypress Avenue. He has been a fixture in Arlanza for many years. He is "the" barber in Arlanza. Everyone seems to know Mars and he has cut the hair of most of the men in the neighborhood for over 40 years. His barbershop is located in what is believed to be the Camp Anza finance office building. Mars was a great help to the author as this book was being researched. (Courtesy Frank Teurlay.)

Lina Hernandez Martinez (pictured on page 50), a former Camp Anza laundry employee, stands in front of the former laundry building. Lina worked for 30 years in the Alvord School District in the Head Start program. She and her husband, Frank, still live near the former Camp Anza property. (Courtesy Frank Teurlay.)

Goodrich Aerostructures has since acquired Rohr. They are currently producing the inner barrel inlet for the 787 engine. The inlet barrel is the dark area just inside the 787 engine seen here. This photograph shows a test engine attached to a 777 body for performance testing. (Courtesy Goodrich Aerostructures.)

The project group that worked on the 787 engine inlet barrel is pictured here in Area 41 of the Riverside plant. (Courtesy Goodrich Aerostructures.)

This 1980s photograph shows the expansion of the Rohr plant. Area 41, where the 787 work is now done, appears on the right center portion of the picture. In the foreground, all remnants of Girls Town are gone, replaced by a strip mall, apartments, and single-family homes. (Courtesy Goodrich Aerostructures.)

Clara Teurlay, the author's mother, started work at Rohr Aircraft Corporation in March 1956 and moved to Arlanza in 1960. She continues to work at Goodrich after 52 years of service. During that time, she raised three sons as a single parent, was the secretary of the Arlanza Little League, and now portrays Mrs. Santa Claus at the annual Goodrich employee Christmas event. (Courtesy Frank Teurlay.)

The author and his younger brother, Charles, are seen here feeding the Girls Town ponies. Though the trees in the distance, former Camp Anza buildings can be seen. Around 1962, a few feet from where this picture was taken, the author found a rusty, broken horseshoe buried in the dirt. After assuming it must have come from a cowboy's horse passing through a hundred years earlier, it seemed for a moment like a historic relic worth keeping. But it was rusty and broken and didn't quite look right, so it was thrown away. Many years later, upon finding the photograph below in the National Archives, a whole new perspective on that old horseshoe emerged. The horseshoe was not from a horse, it had belonged to the men who served at Camp Anza. (Above, courtesy Clara Teurlay; below, courtesy NARA.)

This photograph appeared on the last page of the last issue of the *Anza Zip*. It is fitting that it appears on the last page of this book as well. It shows Camp Anza in the final days of its existence. From this time on, a new chapter would be written. Instead of just passing through, people came to live, build homes, and raise families. (Courtesy Riverside Public Library.)

Col. Walter Johnson, the father of Camp Anza and grandfather of Arlanza, lived in Riverside until his passing in 1961. He now lies in the Fort Rosecrans National Cemetery in San Diego. This image is a reminder that we owe a debt of gratitude to those previous generations who made tremendous sacrifices during WWII on our behalf. (Courtesy Frank Teurlay.)

ACROSS AMERICA, PEOPLE ARE DISCOVERING SOMETHING WONDERFUL. *THEIR HERITAGE.*

Arcadia Publishing is the leading local history publisher in the United States. With more than 4,000 titles in print and hundreds of new titles released every year, Arcadia has extensive specialized experience chronicling the history of communities and celebrating America's hidden stories, bringing to life the people, places, and events from the past. To discover the history of other communities across the nation, please visit:

www.arcadiapublishing.com

Customized search tools allow you to find regional history books about the town where you grew up, the cities where your friends and family live, the town where your parents met, or even that retirement spot you've been dreaming about.